Sports Illustrated KIDS

MY FIRST BOOK OF BASKETBALL

High low five!

Low high five!

A ROOKIE Book

By Beth Bugler and Mark Bechtel

Illustrations by Bill Hinds

Basketball is a super-fast game played by

TWO TEAMS

that try to score points by shooting
a ball through a basket.

Each team puts

FIVE PLAYERS

on the court at a time.

Don't smile.
Don't smile.
Don't smile.

Let's change your jersey numbers to 1 through 5.

The game is divided into

FOUR QUARTERS

that are **12 MINUTES** long.

After the second quarter, the teams take a

HALFTIME

break so the players can rest.

And the fans can make a pit stop?

Basketball is played on a

COURT.

At each end is a
BASKET that has a round **RIM**
attached to a **BACKBOARD.**

I like the size of this little court.

FREE THROW LINE

THREE-POINT LINE

SIDELINE

BASELINE

The five team members have different duties.

POINT GUARD: A little guy with a big job. He's like a coach on the court, telling players what to do.

SHOOTING GUARD: A good scorer who can shoot the ball through the basket.

SMALL FORWARD: A versatile player who needs to be big and strong, but also quick.

POWER FORWARD: A big, tough guy who can score and also guard opposing players.

CENTER: Usually the tallest guy on the team. He tends to hang out near the basket.

QUARTER

1ST

The team that has the *ball* is called the

OFFENSE.

The team that is trying to stop them from scoring is called the

DEFENSE.

TIME
10:28

What? Did you think I wasn't going to catch it?

I don't think I can throw a ball that far.

Players move the ball around by throwing a

PASS

to a teammate.

The offense can also move the ball around the court by

DRIBBLING.

A player bounces the ball up and down with one hand.

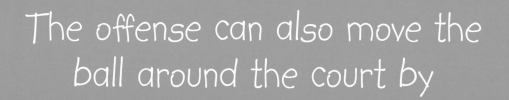

The offense has to shoot the ball before the

SHOT CLOCK

runs out. In men's games, that's 24 seconds. In women's games, it's 30.

He puts up a shot. Will it go in?

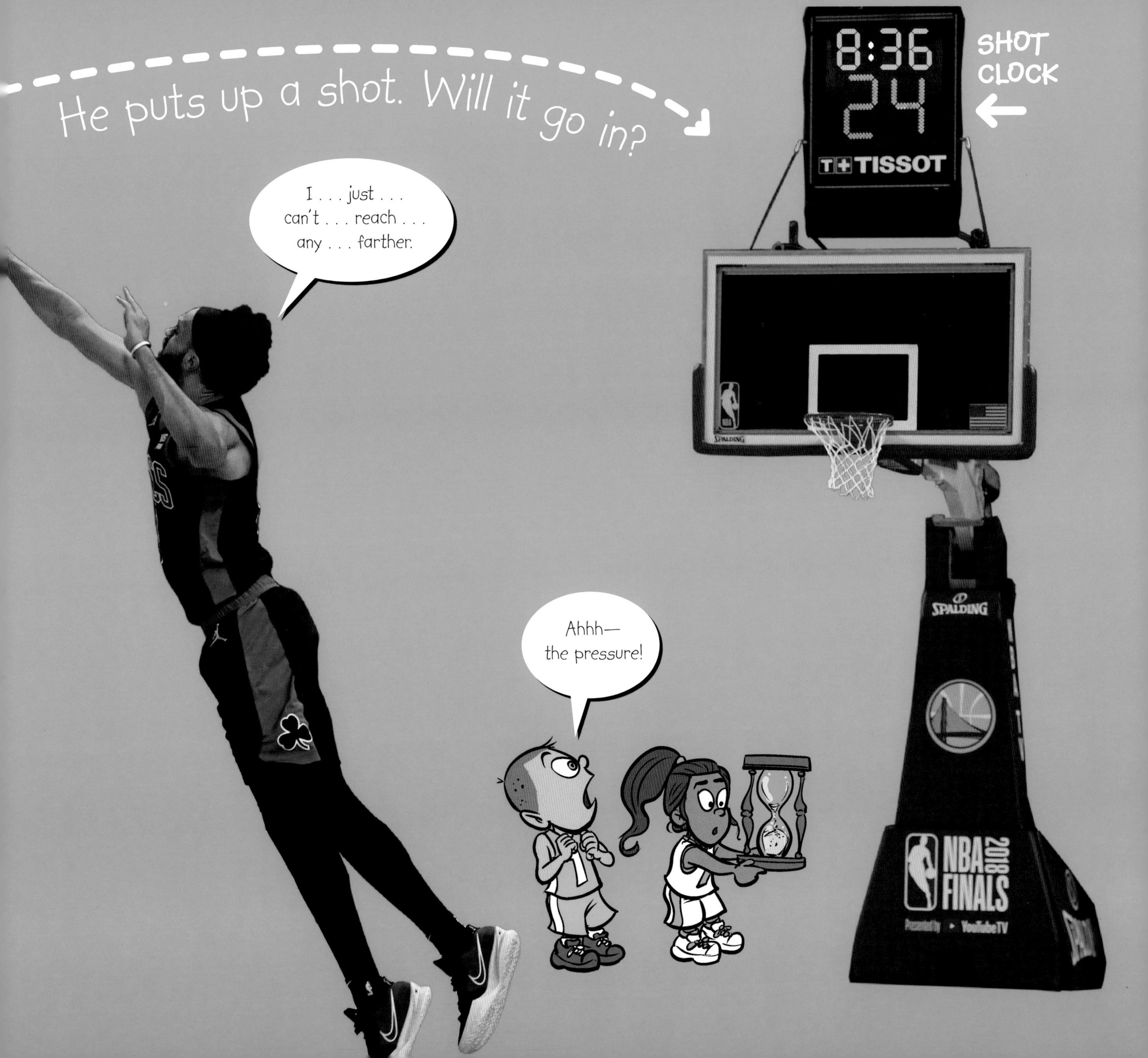

No! The shot clangs off the rim.
Now the players try to grab the

REBOUND.

A defensive player snatches the ball,
and now her team is on offense.

I guess I could
have tried to
grab it, too.

Looks good!

The team that gave up the basket now gets possession of the ball behind the baseline. They have to make an

INBOUNDS PASS.

TIME
3:49

I'm open!

It's a new quarter and a guard is dribbling the ball up the court.

Coach is going to be so disappointed in me.

11:33

Look out! The defensive player reaches in and takes the ball away. It's a

STEAL!

Just **try** and get this away from me.

But you have to be careful when you're trying for a steal. If one player makes too much contact with another, the referee will blow the whistle and call a

FOUL.

TWEET! TWEET!

TIME
8:57
So NOT gentle!
I'll just gently reach in there . . .
LAKERS
6
bibigo
I'm not touching you. I'm not touching you.

Certain fouls lead to

FREE THROWS.

The player who was fouled shoots from the free throw line, and the defensive players can't guard her.

A free throw that goes in the basket is worth one point.

You know what else is free? A hug!

Since he's behind the
three-point line, the shot is a

THREE-POINTER.

It's worth an extra point if it goes in!

:54

Yes! Three points!

BZZZZZZZ!

There's the buzzer.
That means it's . . .

We're back in action.
A player is taking a shot
near the basket.

But the defensive team's center
comes over and

BLOCKS

the shot.

He knocks the
shot away!

QUARTER

3RD

Somebody looks like he's getting tired. It's time for a

SUBSTITUTION.

Anytime there's a break in play, a new player can come onto the floor and replace a teammate.

I got you, bro.

TIME
8:22

If we sit here, maybe they will accidentally send us in.

Play starts up again. The referee calls

GOALTENDING.

That's when a player knocks away a shot that is on its way down into the basket. You can only block a shot when the ball is on the way up.

The referee blows his whistle and the shot counts as a made basket.

Uh-oh. This guy doesn't agree with the referee's call. He complains too much, and the referee calls a

TECHNICAL FOUL.

The other team gets to shoot a free throw.

When I complain too much, I get sent to my room.

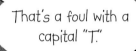

QUARTER

4TH

A player grabs a loose ball and starts dribbling as fast as she can toward the other team's basket. It's a

FAST BREAK.

Her teammates run with her, and the defense tries to catch up. Will they get her?

Whew! So this is why Coach makes us run so many sprints.

No! It's a

SLAM DUNK!

He rises up and stuffs the ball through the hoop!

Wow.

How does he get down from there?

QUARTER
4TH

It's getting late and the game is close. The coach calls a

TIMEOUT.

The players gather around and the coach draws up a play.

They go back on the court.

Look! My play has a dragon!

TIME
:23
I want to hear more about that dragon play.
We've been over this play a thousand times. You remember, right?
Ugh. This play again?
Oh yeah! My favorite play!

It's a **BUZZER BEATER.**

You're the man!

Take that Mr. Clock!

YES!

The two points give her team the win!

GAME OVER!

It's time to celebrate!

YAY!

I thought this might come in handy!

Sports Illustrated KIDS

Library of Congress Cataloging-in-Publication Data available upon request.

Printed in China
ISBN 978-1-63727-527-6

This book is available in quantity at special discounts for your group or organization. For further information, contact:
Triumph Books LLC
814 North Franklin Street
Chicago, Illinois 60610
(312) 337-0747
www.triumphbooks.com

PHOTO CREDITS, in order
Page 1: John W. McDonough; Page 2: Jeffery A. Salter; Page 3: Sipa via AP Images; Page 6: John W. McDonough; Pages 8-9: Dustin Bradford/Getty Images; Page 10: David E. Klutho; Page 11: David E. Klutho; Page 12: Chris Keane; Page 13: Cole Burston/Getty Images; Pages 14-15: John W. McDonough; Pages 16-17: Erick W. Rasco; Page 18: Christian Petersen/Getty Images; Page 19: AP Photo/Evan Vucci; Pages 20-21: Sipa via AP Images; Page 22: Greg Nelson; Page 23: John W. McDonough; Pages 24-25: Olivia Vanni/The Herald via AP; Page 26: Greg Nelson; Page 28: Chris Williams/Icon Sportswire via AP Images (Chuck); Bob Rosato (Hugo); John Fisher/CSM via AP Images (Bango); Page 29: David E. Klutho; Page 30: Greg Nelson; Page 32: AP Photo/Nick Wass; Page 33: AP Photo/Nick Wass; Page 35: David E. Klutho; Page 37: Greg Nelson; Page 39: M. Anthony Nesmith/Icon Sportswire via AP Images; Page 41: Greg Nelson; Page 43: Rich von Biberstein/Icon Sportswire via AP Images; Page 44: AP Photo/Nam Y. Huh; Page 45: Melissa Tamez/Icon Sportswire via AP Images; Page 46: M. Anthony Nesmith/Icon Sportswire via AP Images; Back cover: David E. Klutho.

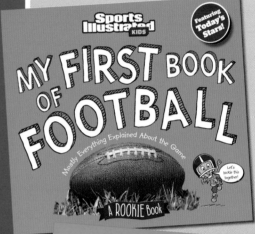
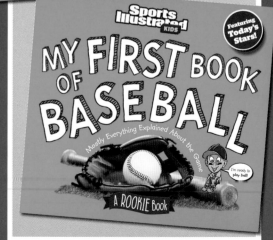